GIRL IN A FOREST

Girl in a Forest
by Elline Lipkin

TRIO
HOUSE
PRESS

Copyright © October 01, 2025 Elline Lipkin

No part of this book may be used or performed without written consent of the author, if living, except for critical articles or reviews.

Lipkin, Elline
1st edition

ISBN: 978-1-949487-60-2
Library of Congress Control Number: 2025933302

Interior design by Natasha Kane
Cover design by Joel W. Coggins
Author photo by Sylvia Gunde
Editing by Natasha Kane

Trio House Press, Inc.
Minneapolis
www.triohousepress.org

For David and Nicole Lipkin

&

for Marigold Street

all paths that lead home

TABLE OF CONTENTS

Leaving   3

I. Girl Lost

Gretel: Looking Back   7
Mother: In the Earth   8
Witch: I Wanted Children   9
The House Speaks   10
Hansel: It Was Put Upon You   12
Mother: Unwell   13
Father: Couvade   15
Mother: As We Were   16
The Woodcutter   17
Stepmother   19
Witch: Potion   20
Wartology   21
Gretel: Home Again   22
Gretel: Brother   23
Witch: Grimoire   24
Husband: Hart   25
Mother: Realizes   26
Mother: Daughter   28
Gretel: Motherless Daughter   29
Mother: Reversed   30
Gretel: Considers   31
Gretel: Grimoire   32
Dear Gretel,   33
Last Blood   34

II. Girl Trapped

Gretel: Older   37
Amulet: Rose Quartz   38
Gretel: While the Children Went to School   39
The Onionskin Paper   40

Amaryllis, Forcing Jar	41
Lunar	42
Witch: Younger	43
Temper	44
Witch: What I Was	45
Fingernail Moon	46
Windowsill, Paperwhite	47
Mirror: Mirror	48
Spirits	49
Mother: Raving	50
Mother: Have Mercy	51
Witch: I Was Marked	52
Poem in Which the Subject Does Not Appear	54
Father: Serpent's Tooth	55
Witch: Once, I Was	56
She Got Pretty Far	57
Middled	58
Forest, Forest, Gone	59
Boy in Garden, Photo Card	60
Girl, Fragments	61
The Wild Blue Rain of June	62
The House Lit from Within	63
Terre Verte	64
Notes	67
Acknowledgments	69
Gratitude	71
About the Author	75

Leaving

The days turn into hours,
hours into minutes,
minutes to moments,
moments, specks

that fly as if from
a tree, unleaving,
each memory
adrift, rattled
by wind, spiraling
downward.

Is this really all
that is left —
the coasting,
some swirl,
a cool breeze,
the momentary
lift before last
landing, before
final fall.

I. Girl Lost

Gretel: Looking Back

Crumbs jostled inside my brother's pocket, worried
    like coins rubbed to plain metal,
        a face soothed, smoothed, then scattered.

Inside my body, I knew I carried two pursefuls,
    on one side, the clasp just opening, ripening,
        readying to let a speck spiral down.

I could see the witch's ribs were a birdcage,
    a flutter beating at the bars like a dying bird
        trying to get out.

From his cell, my brother held out a bone to fool
    he was shriveled. I felt my blood thrumming,
        then ribboning, then rivering.

When I pushed her headfirst into the flames,
    I was the one fattened with power. I had never
        been so blood-sure, so strong.

Mother: In the Earth

I was rootstock, I was dirt, I made myself
        the air surrounding their mouths.
When they lay on the ground, I was a round of moss
        pillowing beneath their sweaty heads.

I willed the loam to cradle their bodies,
        longed to tap a finger from the underside out.
I let the wind say *I am here*.
        I let the night sounds say *try to sleep*.

My bones settled deep beneath the grass.
        I was a mix of motes I tried to waft
into the forest's scent, to close the arms
        of branches almost in embrace.

Witch: I Wanted Children

With thighs like suet
    I could dimple with a pinch,
their dots of fingertips
    tapping at things, half-moon
cheeks smooth as plums
    just bloomed on the cool
side of the tree. A girl
    by my side to sweep the hearth.
A boy who fit to my arms
    as he ran through the door.

Instead, one clogged
    inside me, a garble of blood,
sinew knotted like a tangle
    of string, then emptied
my body like a lost balloon.
    It trickled my legs until
one last spasm, then
    I knew the wraith had left
to haunt another womb.

I drank a tea of nettles.
    I steeped rue, crushed
columbine inside my wine.
    A draught with pennyroyal
pushed the last thorn out.
    A blood-dark tincture
became my potion.

So, when I spied them
    happy, deep in the woods,
my middle twitched.
    One bite, I thought,
just a swallow. My lips itched
    to have that taste of hope
so deep inside again.

The House Speaks

Because she wanted it,
        I sugared and slivered,
mapling like a tree
        veined with sticky sap.
My walls latticed like a tart
        woven and streuseled
to lure the boy and girl in.

Inside, I kept a cot for weeping,
        a hall for shucking
mud and angers. A stair wound
        up to an attic, packed like
a headache ready to pound.
        The hearth beat my furious heart —
embered, then poked,
        drafting up the chimney's nose,
while the kettle wept its tears.

She kept me, or I kept her.
        The windows whisper-smeared,
the floorboards clacked and tapped.
        Some nights my shoulders fell a little,
trying to wrap the heat deeper
        around her like a childhood quilt.
She talked to me. I shuddered back.

So, when I saw her go head first
        into the oven, I breathed
deep as the fumes began to waft.
        There was her skirt
poofed to acrid vapor,
        bile charring as
her innards flung out.
        Her loose hair crisped
and singed until she was bald,
        born again into air.

Her clenched hands prickled
        as they clawed up my back
and I swallowed her voice,
        pleading to me as
it crumbled and cracked.

Hansel: It Was Put Upon You

Your sister trailed while you plotted.
Someone had to be in charge.

Pockets thick with stones,
their rough clink to silence fear.

Exiled, you boysplained your plan.
Pebbling bread to dot the forest —

crumbs for latitude, a crust for long,
a palimpsest to map the green.

Still, you were clever, when the witch
caught you, slammed the cage shut,

the chicken bone lean while your fingers
fattened on meat that plumped your back.

No one could see when you cradled
your knees in the corner and wailed,

a child, helpless and trapped.

Mother: Unwell

I walked back to the cottage,
        birch in full leaf, yellows
and oranges poppying the path,
        mushrooms like paving stones
leading to the front door, ground
        now shifting underfoot.

In the hollow of my body
        had been two seeds,
first fed through blood. Rooted
        till rousted, their tendrils
unwound, and all I wanted
        was to wind them back.

Inside our house was a story,
        man, woman, boy, girl,
loyal dog, calm cat, spiders netting
        into the eaves. Two chairs
to rock into the years,
        a hearth where we all fit.

A prick of poison, the doctor said,
        its leach making ash
of my bones. My feet carried me,
        mind sashed with news,
wishing time could sift so
        I could be again unknowing.

I set the table for our supper,
        unbelled the butter, rosette-molded,
cut the bread, oblonged into a fat loaf,
        counted dishes scalloped with
a simple flourish, and laid the long
        knife close to my place.

I smoothed the air before
        the others came back,
thought of last evening's
        calm before now, each morning,
this news would be a dagger
        descending my throat.

First, to my innards, carving
        what was once fertile. Then nicking
my mind just knowing its harm.
        I would swallow its edge,
my tongue along the tip, its glint a vision
        of full spring, their tall heads,

me, again, strong and whole.

Father: Couvade

When a child is born a custom where a father
takes to bed as if bearing the child himself.

The quilt wrapped around we three,
        later, four, warmth stitched
through the batting like the common
        blood tracing our veins.

Bodies so close, the babe
        where once my wife and
I joined. A smell of yeast rising
        from his crown,
now that union made warm.

I cradled both, set my knee over
        the coverlet to weave us
more tightly. Contentment
        tied me, never before

knowing I yearned to be hemmed,
        how the wide bed, its
wooden posts were a border
        that penned us all in.

Mother: As We Were

Once, there was a cottage:
>stone chimney, dirt floor, beds of straw.

Twice, there was a child:
>boy, girl, cradled, porridged, apple-cheeked, held in arms.

Four-sided, we curved to circle, drawstring-cinched,
>husband linking a child on each side.

Three — I am subtracted. Under coverlet, patterned quilt,
>my hands still swim to reach them
>>through the night's smoke and dark.

The Woodcutter

Wife with flaxen hair.
Wife with emerald eyes.

Your breath rattled the dry
gulf of your mouth, tongue
cottoned with half knowing.

Your hands reached
— for what? —
laddering into air.

I opened the window
so, when ready, your soul
could fly out.

Body thin as a matchstick,
I knew one last strike would set it
to vapor, then mound to ash.

I cupped my hands around
what was left and inhaled.

Grief twisted me and I bent,
low, into the hook of another's
arms. Never did I think

she would burn the sheets,
sweep your dust out, cast a maze
to send the boy and girl far.

Never did I think I would be
so weak you had to haunt —

a sound low in my ears,
a twitch at the base of each bone,
where I couldn't bear the flinch.

Never did I think I could do it
— send them to join you —
deep inside the forest's dark.

Stepmother

Underfoot, underway,
little, little, littles.

A broom to sweep them out the door,
a rag to brush away their marks.

A wipe of dirt across the ledge,
a shake to send the imprint from their beds.

He was fine and strong but these two
were barnacles to his knees, dragging.

The girl's silhouette against shadow —
the outline of who once was and would one day be.

At dusk, the boy's bump of nose, plump cheek,
again drew their mother's face against the wall.

A balloon emptied inside my body,
another month of nothing taking root.

They had to go — this grief and flowering
— nothing could grow inside this house.

Witch: Potion

For the girl-speck
    inside her womb
born flecked with
    half-daughters
held at center.

To rid the doubling
   in the blood, and
     what stays,
a taint of cells circulating
      after one body
    splits
       to send
the other one out.

Wartology

One on the chin,
    thimble left at the edge of the sewing table,
        shrunk down and stuck. Capped by thread
            for the white dress still never sewn.

One on the forehead,
    brow unsmoothed, roughened, three lines fencing across,
        cross-hatched by elevens between the eyes.
            Round and ragged, impediments on a path.

There on her neck,
    like a button at the back of a marionette
        on/off for what could be said and then silenced.
            A Braille glyph left unread, polka dot top.

Again, on her hand,
    what did it touch? Mushrooming up.
        What tunneled beneath shriveled palm,
            bent digits, crumpled reach

                around so much never grasped.

Gretel: Home Again

My legs had been green wood,
bending and pliant, able to leap
and land and never snap.
My voice had been little-kid

thick, budding vowels as
I sang, unashamed, to the forest,
like star jasmine sweetening
the night's cusp of air.

Hair, a tangle of pollen and twigs
clouding my ears like powder
just tapped. Unbrushed, to keep
a wildness before I'd have to tame

it down my back, molting innocence
to quiet sheen. Two cloves curled
inside my flat chest, ticking beneath
gingham, pressed against my dress.

Once back, father and brother slept
near the iron bar they laid inside
the oak door. Outside, the pines
now sentried the front walk.

But in that motherless house
I still couldn't sleep. It wasn't fear
that rattled the windowless dark.
It was knowing harm was a wind

that could sweep through
the eaves. I washed and I washed,
but when I looked down,
red still shadowed my hands.

Gretel: Brother

o' mine
        what sadness settled in your little boy bones.

We were in it together, like twins,
        same peas, one pod,

we were brave, you were clever,
        led me on, ran fast.

My braid tailed behind my back,
        your feet, like arrows, pointed far.

I saved us but your map led us back,
        crumbs like tacks pinning the path.

It was years ago. And now we are three,
        sitting at the table with memories

of which we won't speak. One day,
        we'll tree again, the branch dividing.

This root — how our
        lives were lost and saved —

is an ash we cannot
        swallow, stays on our plates.

Witch: Grimoire

To eat a plump limb,
        to gnaw the rich marrow,
to take them inside my body,

to taste the moments
        before they lost innocence,
the bitter and the sweet.

Husband: Hart

The deer was fleet and fast
    and rummaged the forest,
a bristle riffling the leaves
    as it swept by. There was
a fawn and a doe, its
    belly curving new kin,
jelly forelegs folded tight
    into a ball, just starting to form.

It posed and I shot, then
    my knife carved it to parts,
now hanging from ropes
    in the rafters of the cellar.
I gave the meat to
    my wife. I took the heart
for myself, four folds of
    muscle, chambered

separate but close.
    One, I thought,
for the doe now
    without her mate;
one for the child without
    its mother; one for
the unborn just stirring
    inside. One for myself.

I tried to say it was
    right, natural,
to know separation,
    grief both sustenance
and sorrow. It was the meal
    we ate each night.

Mother: Realizes

I never dreamed I wouldn't
    wake to their heads, round
    as mushroom caps,
flaxen, birch, or husband's hair,
    fragrant as heartwood.

Not see the dough-like puffs
    around their arms and thighs,
smiles just because I came near.
    I thought the path ahead would be
long, pot after pot, each day a road
    that I paved at our hearth then

wound out into the woods, another
    year, another year, another year.
The girl at my knee, boy under my arm.
    I would hold one on each side
until they passed my shoulders,
    left to go beyond our door.

Now, heart stuttering like the wing
    of the moth vibrating by the light
as it burned off, my blood like sludge
    after rain at our front door. I sat
when my pulse thrummed like a river,
    tainted, even as it washed my insides.

I made the bread, I set the table,
    wept as I stood in the stillness
before they were all back,
    tried to fill the room with amber air,
to seal it into the cracks.
    This is the life that was given me.

I would have it all the days that I could,
    cupping a cheek longer than needed
to mold its shape into my hand.
    A rich twilight, the birds still speaking.

I put my hand over my heart. I breathed in the house. I was still here.

Mother: Daughter

A strand
　　of your braid
　wrapped like
　　the whorl
　on a finger
　　or a coil
　of a tress
　　or a curl
　that once latticed
on the babe's
　　globe of a head,
my whole world.

Gretel: Motherless Daughter

Finally, the body was bundled,
    round face peeping out
like a glow worm that crawled
    up my arm.

My legs still shook after the long night,
    blood pooling in the basin set between them.
The moon through the window was
    a pearl eye fixing me in its stare.

The midwife came from down
    the road, my husband outside, barred,
wept with worry. There was the girl
    who fetched things from the kitchen:

tinctures, cloths, clear water.
    On vigil. There was constant scurry.
But I wanted my mother,
    and she wasn't there.

It was me and the babe, falling
    through the hours, each wave
like a doorstep where I balanced
    then slid, not knowing how to

land. A spiral of hard dark.
    I gasped to find any footing,
tided again and again into
    the next wave.
If only I had your hand.

Mother: Reversed

The earth had just started to carpet,
    wisps of sprouts, a fuzz of green,
bounce of grass long enough to bend.

Against a warm rock, my daughter lifted
    her skirt so the sun could warm her thighs.

There were birds chirping, yes, a warm breeze,
    and I could see dandelions drift through air.

I was a creak inside a box, an elbow against
    breaking slats. Earth in my mouth tasted metal,
a musk enveloped, as molecule by molecule,

I shrank. Level in the earth, my hands leached
    into loam, cradled by stillness as I sank.

I knew my girl was roaming. She would meet
    creatures bounding into spring, and one day,
beckon someone into the tall grass.

Gretel: Considers

When I thought of my mother,
        I pictured a hand twined
into the roots of an oak,
        reaching up from below,
            fingers knobbed
like the knot she made each night
        tying up the mood of the house.

She ribboned a peace around
        the walls while my brother
and I slept, wove a thin streamer
        into our dreams,
soothed father's dark mood
          — a ripple that stirred
the dark into the other room.

I went to the spot to think of it —
        pulling the grass like a blanket
up to my cheek, imagined that
        strange relief — to be unseen.
My brother or father, two left to link,
    I wondered how they would match,
        two divided from four, a sum half gone.

I pulled my leg out. I kissed the place
   where her head once was.
      I breathed into the dusk. Turned to
the house again, its square window-eyes,
    mouth-door, front tongue of a walk,
that curved the way in. I tried to carry her spirit,
      make the house warm,
   to carry the mist in my arms.

Gretel: Grimoire

To rend the veil between us,
    stir in sweat from the bed
where you flailed last,

window cracked so your soul
    could escape.

A gray-blonde strand
    left on the pillowcase,
moon-sun, rays, fanning

your head, a penumbra as you
    entered that endlessness.

Dear Gretel,

I wore a darkness
        that laced and latticed,
interleaved my hair,
        its dusk like a ribbon,
    velvet, yet torn.

I tied it at my throat,
        let it knot and tangle
    the edge of my dress,
  unhemmed into scallops
        drooping and raw.

It brushed at my knees,
   a shadow that
      chased like a haint
 as I ran. That old anger
      bridled and bucked,

I let it ride on my back
        until I found a way home.

Last Blood

Riven, rift,
  a weave split, I was sure inside
    was nothing but black.

     Once, I was a girl, a drop
       beaded my thigh like a red
         gem meant for a first necklace.

       Now, I housed a hinterland,
         innards like a field scraped
           to show rotted seeds left in arid soil.

         But no, that sudden stab a shock
           just like that first slap, then stain
             then splodge, now flood again.

           Something had to still show itself,
             a churn of my guts to say this will stop.
            Nights with my hips swaddled,

              these humors again gathering,
              bloodsure, a pounding, like a
                 storm that has to rain itself out.

II. Girl Trapped

Gretel: Older

I was a good wife
and even better doe,
complacent, observing,
a cold nose tipped in
through the open window,
kissing you welcome,
a flank preened for petting
as I readied to wreath
your feet warm.

I was the row of cups
lining the shelves, handles
like ears turned to catch
your growls or a sudden stomp,
a hand slammed into
the wood that said your
supper wasn't still warm.

I was the coverlet, the batting,
the ticking, zigzag stitch
joining the scraps like a map.
A zipper of thread basting
an old patch with the last sheen
of my wedding dress. A throat
of color torn off the bolt.

I was the moon peering in,
animal, mineral, elemental,
the cabin like a trap that you
set after you slipped into the
early dark while I tried to sleep,
seeing the trees lace above
the roof, saying again,
there is always a way out.

Amulet: Rose Quartz

Pale, translucent,
noctilucent, set
against the table's
opaque black.

Stone of flourish,
stone of longing,
a pink to cup
against the lines
of one palm.

Jasper, jade, and
onyx, each dark
a base holding
in its angers.

Pale like dawn
peeling from
the grip of night,
a swarm of marble
feelings set
inside a storm.

Gretel: While the Children Went to School

I baked the bread.
I washed the sheets.
I sat with my cups,
read a little from the
small bookshelf.
The cat wreathed my feet
until I picked her up.

I swept the hearth.
I boiled the water. Was
excited when it was time
for them to come home,
running through the door
like sun bolting through
panes of glass.

They crawled back
into my lap and I pulled
their heads close to see
the whorl at each crown
spiraling like a climbing star.
One in each arm,

they made the chain I needed,
sinking my feet into the floor.
I tended them like flowers,
wanting the bloom to last.
Cuttings and hulls, I swept
to the corners. For now,

we were a nimbus rising
inside the cabin, stripes
of light incandescing
as we bent over the desk,
warmth pulsing between us
before their father came back.

The Onionskin Paper

is still in the night table drawer,
with typed advice for marriage.
Thin paper, preserved, a benison
stamped by the typewriter,
as the letters now fray into fiber,
and overlay onto a half century,
that ecru bond deepening to heirloom,
talisman, guardian, the border of years.

Amaryllis, Forcing Jar

Thin twine of roots,
   floss like the limbs
of a fetus, translucent
   and floating
underwater.
   Green just about
to blade out,
   an edge daring
again against
   the belled glass.

Lunar

> *What if the moon was never a beautiful woman?*
> *— Katha Pollitt*

The fat moon hangs full,
        incandescing on a low black shelf,

its lambent hull ambering
        the day's dregs into quiet scree.

It is the ripe milkmaid's loosed button,
        wandering eye of a little girl lost,

tide keeping time to pace 28,
        Cleopatra's last uncrushed pearl.

A nacreous wrap around the stars'
        least grit, secret teeth enameling

dust to blanched stone.
        Bald and shiny, the moon tints

with pure longing, a thrown pill sent to
        orbit from the cabinet's flung door.

Witch: Younger

My voice a knife,
a slash, aslant,
the one weapon
concealed
and carrying.
When I was told
(often) how piercing,
how harsh,
I learned
to swallow its tip.

One sharp tack
closed my throat,
its edge beveling
my words, a glint
in each tone.
My tongue laved rage,
though it sounded
like a thin whisper.

Sometimes
a bitter drip
molted inside
my throat,
made vulture
into voice, and
a claw reached
up to strangle
from within.

Temper

> *v. to exercise control over:* GOVERN, RESTRAIN; *calmness of mind,* COMPOSURE, EQUANIMITY; *heat of mind or emotion, passion.*

Silence was the salt within her speech, crusting words
to an edge, so they walled inside a lattice.

Her moonstone eyes flashed, called "opal jewels,"
"delicate," as each orb whorled into an annihilating

blank. The divan held the press of her figure,
an outline of a self, hemmed and settled,

pinned straight. Offered an anodyne for rage,
a swallow sealed her throat like a dank clamp.

Witch: What I Was

That single bud,
yearning my neck
just over the glass,
meant to drink water,
root upward, through
a center stalk. Not
a sip, never a demand.

The vase placed in
the corner, silent, admired,
to unpetal slowly,
(and be what falls off),
lilac blending into white,
until the viscous rot
at the bottom also
becomes a source of scent.

I was meant to be
that decorative,
never an intrusion.
Yet, the thorn's
spiny-edge, a hardness
at the root. I muted —
a belligerent red turned
carmine-cured, steeped
a rich, insouciant black.

Fingernail Moon

    Tonight, a thin cusp cups the vast black,
        a silver rim thimbling
            stars into strewn seams.

    Its demi-gape is a moaned O, a half gasp,
        a belly pressed flat
            to hold its small store.

    Below, the dark spills its rich infinite,
        a low curve contracting
            around all it still doesn't have.

Windowsill, Paperwhite

Knobby onion,
with crisped outer
edges peeling
a thin scrim
around circles
that unripple
tight to cinch
the center seed
Matroushka'd
deep within.

Quiet in water,
until white hair
begins to drown
a Medusa's head
tipped and dowsing,
tangling its snakes,
while thin green legs
bean up in pairs
as the glass holds
their hips, forced.

The burst is sudden,
star-whitening,
a petaled shoe worn
for a week now
kicking off wafts
of civety musk
enveloping air
so that heads turn,
not knowing
from where.

Mirror: Mirror

She folds her face up inside the circle,
        open, shut,
a blink while it is snapped back.

The semblance on the other side,
        is pocketed, pursed,
a twin clicked inside the clasp.

A lost soul, a saved scrap,
        visage carried and blotted,
lines blurred, then rubbed out.

The desire is evenness, parchment,
        to again re-blank.
Each caught angle tucked again in.

Spirits

> *Daphne with her thighs in bark.*
> *— Eavan Boland*

In the woods, a girl slipped
        into trees, between shadows
           that fell as her feet
    sank into moss.

A braid of leaftop crowned
        her stillness,
           a chain of green
        garlanded her hair.

Dusk cottoned the dark,
        a scrim of brume
           misting grisaille
        like an atomizer into air.

I saw her standing,
        arms V'ed,
           legs triangled wide
        caught at the waist

in the oak's deep crotch.
        That knot on the trunk
           was an O
    set in silent scream.

Mother: Raving

The woman is entombed,
body flat, plinthed,
as even as the line
bisecting the earth.

Stillness is easy now —
head pillowed on stone,
neck crenellated between slabs.

Too late to Rapunzel,
more needed than
a finger's prick.

Quiet, prone, her body
no longer needed.
The forest is now inside
her hair, a woods rippling

around her eyes, rings
of loss, rings of years,
as a wildness overgrows
the edges of her mouth.

Hands emptied, a last
febrile light dims out,
though a word, plosive,
stays trapped behind her teeth,

now ivoried inside her mouth.

Mother: Have Mercy

> *The woman is perfected. / Her dead //*
> *Body wears the smile of accomplishment...*
> *— Sylvia Plath*

When I came to the altar
   of all I would never have —
a long plank's last step,
   the cut tongue of a lost road
sheared to edge nothing —
   I knew, at last, I was
where I belonged.

I statued, my insides thinned,
   then hollowed as my eyes
softened back to uncarved blanks.
   Arms, now driftless feathers,
quieted, folded back from
   their outstretched reach.

Feet seem to be saying:
We have come so far, it is over.

My back cradled into a wrap
   of dirt, knit of skin
leaching into sediment, each
   opened stitch a ravel of dissolve.
I waited to become vapor, a wisp
   then waft, to be one less scent
impressed into the air.

Let me float to where each
   seed-child went, Mosesed,
basketed, nestled in rushes
   loosening as they drift,
rivering to where everything
   once started, the water's head,
the water's mouth, pouring freely.

   Carry my bones back to that source.

Witch: I Was Marked

Almost sixteen, smooth
cheeked, budding rose, fresh dew.
You know the metaphors.

It was winter, frigid air,
fire a dart of red, a lick of orange,
I wanted so badly to press against heat.

Closer, a dare, just a wisp of touch,
I needed to feel enveloped, to be
inside the wreath smouldering out.

The fire reached for me. I nodded
until my mother's hand yanked
at the nape of my dress.

But I took its mark, my forehead
emblazoned with a jagged bolt
branded down to my brows.

A blight, some say, a sign,
said others. I unpinned my hair,
until it fanned my waist,

twisted a curl around my fourth
finger before it scorched off.
I left, traipsing, yes,

into the proverbial woods,
uncarved from beauty
back to the block of who

I once was, greenwood,
quick-sapped, legs like
a riot of roots tangling

in grass. I let my face
be stamped and scarred
by the wind and rough earth.

The long years embossed
my burned skin like a wax seal
raised on a closed envelope —

a finger over each ridge
marked my losses.
Spelled out my address.

Poem in Which the Subject Does Not Appear

siblings

Empty years	stain	a silence
once whitened	with unknowing	hiding
in even spaces	gaps	instead
secret	easy	billows
the	ransacked	future
a set	now leached	to seeded dregs
each	draught	the taste
	of ruin.	

Father: Serpent's Tooth

> *How sharper than a serpent's tooth it is to have a thankless child!*
> *— Shakespeare*

A crenellated blade's edge,
serrated knife tip, so smooth
you never feel it go in.

That girl turning her back,
that flash of anger, white-hot
a legacy, my own.

Witch: Once, I Was

silk-haired, vellum-skinned,
   a pale page before
starting to scry. Wasp-waist
   belled by hips just jutted to
curve out. Beneath my neck,
   a V cleaved, then upside-
downed beneath layers of tulle.
   My toes pointed sharp inside
polished boots, and I clicked
   to hear them stomp.
I could quartz my eyes
   into a stare that meant
getting what I wanted.
   Admiration was a silk
tight around my neck.

   When the blight came, it
was sudden, a rake clawed
   my forehead and left its mark.
A caul pulled over my beauty,
   hazy what I even wanted,
but that day was an abyss.
   I raged to find a way out,
went into the woods,
   swore I'd live where no one
would see me: wretch,
   wrecked, removed, alone.

She Got Pretty Far

Her mud-streaked boots
      still in the front hall,
stopped before entering
      the house and
         its rich mess.
Her coat, empty,
      on the hook,
   still keeps some
      of her form.

Middled

Deadheaded, the bushes now
just barely line the drive.
Stalks and stems that once
tipped to blooms now point —
blunt, blatant, witchified
sticks, each a finger slashed
to rheumatoid grasp.

The pink, padded flesh is gone,
macheted against the far blue.
We park by their side, slump a little.
In this stark decade, will we have it,
that U-turn back to happiness?

Forest, Forest, Gone

The woods flourished then slid,
    lollipop-topped, leafing then leaving
        bark stark, finger-thin by late fall.

The ground mossed as it spread over loam,
    almost a tide greening like lace
        mottled and mâchéd into soil.

The spirits fled and flit, sprite or haint,
    a green Pan cap left to branch
        while the body tamped under roots,

slipped deeper in dirt, mounded, chambered,
    decayed and mulched, a pause
        in the air, an echo of scent then gone.

Boy in Garden, Photo Card

In the center square, a three-year-old, posed,
one hand on a plastic yellow wheelbarrow,
contrapposto. Pink pull-on garden boots,
an arm sent out, petaled flower in hand.
Angel's trumpets cradle his ears, their sweetness
a vapor alight within the child's fine hair.

This year's card is a yardstick, a flip-book,
a next line on a doorframe measuring height.
The boy taller in increments. Evidence sent
to faraway family. It says, once, we had
one frame of happiness. See the lush garden,
sturdy boy, flowers bend down to meet him.

Girl, Fragments

Shucked stockings left by a bush,

    torn slip lipped on top of a fence,

lace deranged, asymmetric, dragged

   across a jagged rock.

That rich skin

     taut as rigged canvas,

  a seam, a curl, loosed

        to better run.

    A rocket straining against its straps.

     Pleasure. Danger.

   Humming the same roar.

The Wild Blue Rain of June

Gold between trees
      like brushstrokes in a painting
            tipping in sheen.

Heliotrope, hyacinth,
      air flecked with the scent
            released after spring.

A green thicket wraps to
      a porch and open door,
            light bending in to reach the back wall.

Inside, furrows of beds, white cotton
      and wool, a swaddle of muslin,
            and the close weave of arms.

Heat will cinch the air until
      the trees lean into each other
            and everything wraps into kin,

unknitting again in fall. For now, globes
      of hydrangeas proffer their heads,
            radiating scent.

Lilac and salvia, cones of delphiniums,
      the yellow tongue of the iris
            stripes its reach out.

Mist prisms iridescent as the house
      shimmers in relief
            against summer sky.

The House Lit From Within

All I ever wanted
    was to live inside
those radiant squares

beaming from each wall,
    like a vessel built
with gold blocks.

A window lamp
    like a lighthouse beam
beaconing the waves

of dark, moting
    the air with
an aura of calm.

Night like a cipher,
    a thick soil, heavy blanket,
pressing everything down.

While in the house, a halo
    glows around each chair,
cushioning and welcoming.

A circle cast so ease
    can well up to its rim.
To say no matter

how long or
    how lost, the house waits,
a path still leads back.

Terre Verte

> *Translated as 'green earth' a color used by artists since antiquity.*
> *Medieval Italian painters used green earth for underpainting middle*
> *and shadow flesh tones.*

Girl in a forest,
   girl on a lawn,
legs a whir against
   a shadow of loam.

Inside the canvas
   green tinges below
the albumened
   cup of her cheeks.

Thin arms laid
   down by her sides,
decorous, her veins
   filling with roots.

She will lay
   against the curve
of earth, dress-breath
   billowing to sky.

Notes

The epigraph for the poem "*Father: Couvade*" is taken from the Merriam-Webster dictionary.

The poem "*Gretel: Older*" borrows its opening lines from Vanessa Angélica Villarreal's poem "*I Was a Good Wife.*"

The epigraph for the poem "*Lunar*" is taken from Katha Pollitt's poem "*Metaphors of Women.*"

The epigraph for the poem "*Temper*" is taken from the Merriam-Webster dictionary.

The epigraph for the poem "*Spirits*" is the title of Eavan Boland's poem "*Daphne With Her Thighs in Bark.*"

"*Mother: Have Mercy*" incorporates lines from Sylvia Plath's poem "*Edge*" in the epigraph and in its stanzas.

The poem "*Father: Serpent's Tooth*" takes a line from *King Lear* as its epigraph.

The definition of "terre verte" is taken from *The Secret Lives of Color* by Kassia St. Clair.

Acknowledgments

My gratitude to the editors of the publications in which these poems first appeared, at times in earlier versions and with different titles.

Apricity: "*Fingernail Moon*" and "*Lunar*" as "*Pleine Lune.*"

Copper Nickel: "*Gretel: Older*" as "*Self-Portrait, Gretel.*"

Gathering: A Women Who Submit Anthology: "*Witch: What I Was*" as "*Self-Portrait as Angry Flower.*"

Mantis: "*Gretel: Looking Back*" and "*Mother: In the Earth.*"

SWWIM: "*Windowsill, Paperwhite*" as "*Paperwhite.*"

Transformation: *A Women Who Submit Anthology:* "*Poem in Which the Subject Does Not Appear.*"

Gratitude

It might seem unusual to call a single-author book a group project, but without the encouragement and support of so many this book would never have come into existence.

For their deep faith and hard work, I thank editor extraordinaire Natasha Kane, publisher Kris Bigalk, and everyone at Trio House Press.

I thank Molly Peacock who taught my first graduate poetry workshop with such warmth, caring, and commitment, and whose life lived fully as a poet has been an exemplar since. Gratitude to Alice Fulton whose feminist vision has been a beacon and whose reflexive generosity and remembrance have meant so much. Deepest thanks to Jeanne Marie Beaumont who published my first 'fairy tale poem' eons ago in *The Poets Grimm* and whose writing has always served as an inspiration.

Many thanks to Victoria Chang, who knew just what to say to me when. I am so glad for our abiding connection.

I wrote my first poems in response to Sheila Firestone's encouragement and I am grateful to still be in touch and for her example of a life of perpetual learning. Bouquets of flowers to Genevieve Kaplan and Lisa Krueger for hours in the garden and in conversation, for the most essential kind of sustenance. The East Pasadena Poets have been meeting for over ten years and I count myself fortunate to be among them. With gratitude to Linda Dove, Mary Fitzpatrick, Lois P. Jones, Beverly Lafontaine, Mari L'Esperance, Cathie Sandstrom, and *un grand merci* to Judith Terzi.

Poets work with the metaphorical heart, for work with the actual one, I thank Dr. Duc Do. For his compassion, I am grateful to Dr. Andrew Vardanian. For vital time spent together, my ongoing gratitude to Dr. Randi Friedland.

Anchored in our days at Columbia, I am glad for abiding friendships with Jerome Gentes, Nicole Greaves, Scott Hightower, and Kim Rich. The roots of this book reach back to Houston and I am always thankful to my mentors there: Edward Hirsch, Adam Zagajewski, and Cynthia Macdonald.

To Jacsun Shah, so deeply glad to walk alongside each other on this path.

Catherine Park, there aren't words for a connection that transcends them, has lasted so long, and has meant so much. Always, sending deep care, bright hope, and white light.

I am especially grateful to find classmates Blas Falconer and Laura Reece Hogan within the vibrant Los Angeles writing community. And with thanks to Shelley Berger for her abiding faith.

Melisa Cahnmann-Taylor, who propelled me forward, I hope to always be in each other's orbit.

I thank Lee Mellott for her unique support during a critical time. And Elizabeth Silver, who understood so deeply. Karon Jolna and the community at Ms. — it has meant so much to be part of your foundation. There are students from whom I learn as much as I teach and I have been glad to be in the company of my WWLA colleagues and friends for so many years. With special thanks to Buffy Shutt and joy in our connection.

To my father and mother, brother and sister, and all extended family, I am so grateful for your love and support. Thank you to the Horowitz family and to Ellen Reeves, 'extra' in the best sense.

For Marigold Street, which framed our happiness. Where blossoms bent down to meet us. For Athena and Cici. Most of all, for Richard and Leo: everything, always.

About the Author

Elline Lipkin is a poet, nonfiction writer, and academic. She holds an MFA and PhD in Creative Writing and Literature and has been a Postdoctoral Scholar at UC Berkeley and a Research Scholar with UCLA's Center for the Study of Women. Her first book, *The Errant Thread*, was chosen by Eavan Boland for the Kore Press First Book Award. Her second, *Girls' Studies*, is part of the Seal Studies series. She has been in residence at Yaddo, the Virginia Center for the Creative Arts, Dorland Mountain Arts Colony, and was a California Resident at Yefe Nof. A past screener for the Kingsley & Kate Tufts Poetry Awards and mentor for AWP's Writer to Writer program, she is active with WriteGirl in Los Angeles and writes for *Ms.* magazine. For two years, she served her community as Poet Laureate and editor of the *Altadena Poetry Review*.

About the Book

Girl in a Forest was designed at Trio House Press through the collaboration of:

Natasha Kane, Editor and Interior Designer
Joel Coggins, Cover Designer
Sylvia Gunde, Author Photographer

The text is set in Adobe Caslon Pro.

About the Press

Trio House Press is an independent literary press dedicated to discovering, publishing, and promoting books that enhance culture and the human experience. Trio House Press adheres to and supports all ethical standards and guidelines outlined by the CLMP. For further information, or to consider making a donation to Trio House Press, visit us online at triohousepress.org.

www.ingramcontent.com/pod-product-compliance
Lightning Source LLC
Chambersburg PA
CBHW020442090526
44586CB00045B/790